The Character of a Follower of Jesus

DESIGN FOR DISCIPLESHIP

DFD**4**

NAVPRESS®

BRINGING TRUTH TO LIFE

The Navigators is an international Christian organization. Our mission is to advance the gospel of Jesus and His kingdom into the nations through spiritual generations of laborers living and discipling among the lost. We see a vital movement of the gospel, fueled by prevailing prayer, flowing freely through relational networks and out into the nations where workers for the kingdom are next door to everywhere.

NavPress is the publishing ministry of The Navigators. The mission of NavPress is to reach, disciple, and equip people to know Christ and make Him known by publishing life-related materials that are biblically rooted and culturally relevant. Our vision is to stimulate spiritual transformation through every product we publish.

© 1973, 1980, 2006 by The Navigators

All rights reserved. No part of this publication may be reproduced in any form without written permission from NavPress, P.O. Box 35001, Colorado Springs, CO 80935.
www.navpress.com

NAVPRESS, BRINGING TRUTH TO LIFE, and the NAVPRESS logo are registered trademarks of NavPress. Absence of ® in connection with marks of NavPress or other parties does not indicate an absence of registration of those marks.

ISBN 1-60006-007-2

Cover design by Arvid Wallen
Cover illustration by Michael Halbert
Interior design by The DesignWorks Group
Creative Team: Dan Rich, Kathy Mosier, Arvid Wallen, Pamela Poll, Pat Reinheimer, Kathy Guist

Original DFD Author: Chuck Broughton
Revision Team: Dennis Stokes, Judy Gomoll, Christine Weddle, Ralph Ennis

Unless otherwise identified, all Scripture quotations in this publication are taken from the HOLY BIBLE: NEW INTERNATIONAL VERSION® (NIV®). Copyright © 1973, 1978, 1984 by International Bible Society. Used by permission of Zondervan Publishing House. All rights reserved. Other versions used include: The New Testament in Modern English (PH), J. B. Phillips Translator, © J. B. Phillips 1958, 1960, 1972, used by permission of Macmillan Publishing Company; and THE MESSAGE (MSG). Copyright © 1993, 1994, 1995, 1996, 2000, 2001, 2002. Used by permission of NavPress Publishing Group.

Printed in the United States of America

1 2 3 4 5 6 / 10 09 08 07 06

FOR A FREE CATALOG OF NAVPRESS BOOKS & BIBLE STUDIES,
CALL 1-800-366-7788 (USA) OR 1-800-839-4769 (CANADA)

DFD4 | CONTENTS

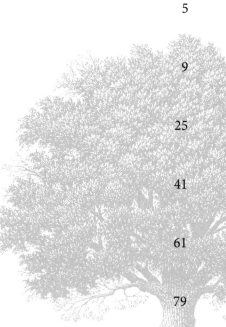

BUILDING FOR QUALITY

Having completed the first three books in the *Design for Discipleship* series, you already know the benefit of personal Bible study — what it means to search the Scriptures and discover Jesus as the Way, the Truth, and the Life. You have probably noticed that responding to God and experiencing His Word affects your attitudes and actions day by day.

However, even though you realize the importance of living out God's Word, you will probably sense opposition. Satan is the enemy of every believer, and he knows the power of God's living Word. He will try to keep you away from it using any method he can. He will suggest such excuses as "You're too busy" or "You can't focus now — do this other thing first and then get back to Bible study later." He will engineer interruptions, temptations, and even criticism by others to hinder you from giving energy and attention to the Scriptures.

Recognizing Satan as a key source of such hindrances reemphasizes the importance of Bible study and can increase your determination to gain victory. How do you win? Here are some practical suggestions:

1. ACCEPT by faith the victory that Christ has already won over Satan and his schemes. "Thanks be to God! He gives us the victory through our Lord Jesus Christ" (1 Corinthians 15:57).
2. ASK the Lord for His wisdom and strength.
3. USE personal discipline to experience God's grace. Just as you must make an effort to keep up your daily quiet time with the Lord, so you must also plan and protect your study time. It is wise to set a definite goal to complete a certain amount of study each week and to be diligent in reaching that goal. "A longing fulfilled is sweet to the soul," Solomon said (Proverbs 13:19), and satisfaction is yours when you reach your objective of devoting regular time with the Lord in His word.
4. ASK friends to encourage you in your weekly Bible study goals, and perhaps share something you have learned with them.

WHY FOCUS ON CHARACTER NOW?

It is so easy to focus on externals and ignore internals. We normally get training for our abilities. But how about our hearts and what's deeper inside? Character flows from within and is defined as "moral excellence and firmness."* God wants to develop in us godly inner qualities as well as outward behaviors.

We will study five areas of character in this course:

- The Call to Fruitful Living
- Authentic Love in Action
- Purity of Life
- Integrity in Living
- Character Development in Suffering

---

* *Webster's New Collegiate Dictionary* (Springfield, MA: G. and C. Merriam Company, 1974).

" The dysfunctions of many [believers] are rooted in a common reality: their capacities have been extensively trained, while their character has been merely presumed.

—Bill Thrall, Leadership Catalyst, Inc.

The Call to Fruitful Living

Many people measure the fruitfulness of their lives by the quantity of their activities. But this does not give a true picture. Who and what you are is more important than what you do. The Bible emphasizes *being* and *character* as you grow to be more like Christ.

GROWING IN THE FRUIT OF THE SPIRIT

1. Read John 15:1-5. Here Jesus gives insight into the matter of spiritual fruit bearing.

   a. In this metaphor, who is the vine and who are the branches?

   b. Why do the branches need the vine?

c. Explain what "remaining in Christ" means to you.

> **❝❝** If Christ lives in us, controlling our personalities, we will leave glorious marks on the lives we touch. Not because of our lovely characters, but because of His.
>
> —Eugenia Price

2. Read about the fruit of the Spirit in Galatians 5:22-23. List the qualities God wants to produce in your life and briefly define each one.

The Fruit of the Spirit	Brief Definition of the Fruit
1.	
2.	
3.	
4.	
5.	
6.	
7.	
8.	
9.	

3. In the Sermon on the Mount, Jesus identified eight basic character qualities for living a full, happy life. For each character quality, list the blessing that Jesus promised (Matthew 5:3-12).

The Blessed Person	Jesus' Promise
1. Is poor in spirit (verse 3)	
2. Mourns (verse 4)	
3. Is meek (verse 5)	
4. Hungers and thirsts for righteousness (verse 6)	
5. Is merciful (verse 7)	
6. Is pure in heart (verse 8)	
7. Is a peacemaker (verse 9)	
8. Is persecuted because of righteousness (verses 10-11)	

4. As the Holy Spirit continues to develop His fruit in your character throughout your lifetime, how will this affect your emotional world?

How will it affect your relationships?

5. Contrast the two types of people in Jeremiah 17:5-8.

The Person Who Trusts in People	The Person Who Trusts in the Lord

6. Consider realistically who and what you usually trust in. What is one area where you need to trust yourself or others less so you can trust God more? Explain.

7. Scripture identifies several important areas of life that reveal our true character. What are they?

Philippians 4:8

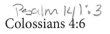

Psalm 141:3

Colossians 4:6

1 Peter 2:12

Ephesians 4:31-32

8. How does the condition of our hearts influence the other parts of our lives? (Luke 6:45)

9. What will happen to your life and mind as you grow in character? (Ephesians 4:22-24)

10. Read James 3:13-18.

   a. How can godly wisdom deepen our character growth?

   b. Contrast godly wisdom with worldly wisdom. (verses 15-17)

Godly Wisdom	Worldly Wisdom

11. Read 1 Peter 1:13-16. What is God's desire for us?

While God is transforming your character to be more like Christ, what are some practical ways mentioned in this passage that you can partner with Him?

12. Let's pause for a moment to reflect. Have you ever tried to change your character on your own, without God's help and grace? What have been the results?

13. Read and meditate on 2 Peter 1:1-8. This portion of Scripture opens up keys to growth in character.

   a. List several things God has provided to help you grow in character. (verses 3-4)

b. Briefly describe the qualities mentioned in verses 5-7.

c. As your character matures in these qualities, how will this both honor God and help you?

d. How have you experienced the power of God changing your character?

e. Try to identify which one of these qualities the Holy Spirit might currently be focusing on in your life. With God's help, what step could you take to become more Christlike in displaying the quality you mentioned?

In what you think:

In what you say:

In how you act:

GROWING IN THE JOY OF HOLY LIVING

14. Read Philippians 3:4-14. Paul experienced deep joy in the process of being transformed by grace.

a. List several of Paul's new attitudes and patterns that differed from his former ones.

Old Attitudes and Patterns (verses 4-7)	New Attitudes and Patterns (verses 7-14)
1. Put confidence in the flesh	
2. Religious leader	
3. Persecuted the church	
4. Blameless in the law	
5. Counted all as profit	

b. Let's look again at verse 13. Paul left some things behind that he had previously depended on for his holy living. What things (if any) are you depending on that you should leave behind?

c. What things are you hoping in as you look forward? (verse 14)

> The contrast between God's way of doing things and our way is never more acute than in this area of human change and transformation. We focus on specific actions; God focuses on us. We work from the outside in; God works from the inside out. We try; God transforms.
>
> —Richard Foster, *Devotional Classics*

15. How did God's grace help Paul grow in character, even in the midst of difficulties and pain? (2 Corinthians 12:7-9)

How has God used hardship to develop you in some aspect of your character?

16. Read John 15:11-16; 16:24; 17:13. From these verses, what will deepen our joy?

What is the key to being filled with joy? (Psalm 16:11)

17. What would a life full of joy look like to you? Have you ever seen someone full of joy and yet weeping? Explain.

18. What did Jesus promise to those who had given up much to follow Him? (Luke 18:29-30)

What is your response to receiving this promise both now and later in heaven?

What we have processed so far is definitely not easy, as our flesh and human tendencies will strongly resist growth. We will also be inclined to do it through our own strength. But our confidence rests in the assurance that God works in us to mature us. In His mercy, our holy God withholds what we justly deserve. He then freely lavishes on us, in Christ, all the grace we need, not only for eternal life but also for our daily lives.

SUGGESTED VERSE FOR MEDITATION AND MEMORIZATION

John 15:5

I am the vine; you are the branches. If a man remains in me and I in him, he will bear much fruit; apart from me you can do nothing.

John 15:5

Write to God about your character. Describe what you see in your character and how you desire to grow in character.

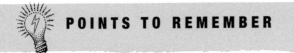

Add a sentence or two to the following statements to summarize the most important things you learned from each section of this chapter.

GROWING IN THE FRUIT OF THE SPIRIT

God desires to develop godly character qualities in our lives as a result of our relationship to Christ.

GROWING IN CHARACTER

Character growth involves thoughts, speech, actions, and emotions.

GROWING IN THE JOY OF HOLY LIVING

God's grace helps us experience joy and grow in character, even in the midst of difficulties and pain.

Do you want to be counted wise, to build a reputation for wisdom? Here's what you do: Live well, live wisely, live humbly. It's the way you live, not the way you talk, that counts. Mean-spirited ambition isn't wisdom. Boasting that you are wise isn't wisdom. Twisting the truth to make yourselves sound wise isn't wisdom. It's the furthest thing from wisdom—it's animal cunning, devilish conniving. Whenever you're trying to look better than others or get the better of others, things fall apart and everyone ends up at the others' throats.

Real wisdom, God's wisdom, begins with a holy life and is characterized by getting along with others. It is gentle and reasonable, overflowing with mercy and blessings, not hot one day and cold the next, not two-faced. You can develop a healthy, robust community that lives right with God and enjoy its results only if you do the hard work of getting along with each other, treating each other with dignity and honor. (James 3:13-18, MSG)

The book of Proverbs gives numerous insights into character growth, especially

> for attaining wisdom and discipline;
>> for understanding words of insight. (Proverbs 1:2)

Consider reading through the book of Proverbs, one chapter a day for the next month. As you read, make a list in your journal of the characteristics of a wise and godly person. You may want to make another column contrasting godly wisdom with the foolishness of worldly wisdom.

2

Authentic Love in Action

" Grace means there is nothing I can do to make God love me more, and nothing I can do to make God love me less. It means that I, even I who deserve the opposite, am invited to take my place at the table in God's family.

—Philip Yancey, *What's So Amazing About Grace?*

1. How did Jesus reveal the greatest love possible? (John 15:12-14)

2. What are some characteristics of genuine love? (1 Corinthians 13:4-8)

What Love Is	What Love Isn't

How is a person affected when he or she receives real love?

3. Carefully read 1 John 4:7-21.

   a. What has God done to demonstrate His love for us?
      (verses 9-10)

   b. What did we do to deserve God's love?

   c. Why should we love? (verses 11,19)

   d. What do you think fear does to love and love to fear? (verse 18)

4. Consider the following statements. Do you tend to agree (A) or
   disagree (D)?

   ____ Love is an action, not an emotion.

   ____ If I give enough love, I do not need to receive love.

____ God is love, He is loving, and He is the jealous Lover of my soul.

____ I don't have to like you, but I do have to love you.

____ Trust is essential both to give and to receive love.

> If equal love there cannot be,
> Let the one who loves the more be me.

—Anonymous

LOVING UNSELFISHLY

Many people have learned only to co-exist with others: "If you do your part," they say, "I'll do mine." This conditional type of giving is not true love. God wants us to say, "I will love you even if I receive nothing in return." God forms this selfless giving and loving in our attitudes and actions. Yet there is another side of this coin. In order to love selflessly, we must have enough energy and fullness to give love. It is from God's love filling us up that we are able to love others unselfishly.

5. Who should followers of Jesus love?

   Deuteronomy 6:5

Luke 6:27

1 Peter 4:8

6. Read John 13:34-35. Why do you think Jesus placed such emphasis on demonstrating love?

7. God created us to have legitimate needs. Read 1 John 3:16-18. What relationship do you see between loving people and meeting their needs?

Why is it important that we allow our own needs to be met by receiving love from others?

 Humility means trusting God and others with you.

—Bill Thrall, Leadership Catalyst, Inc.

8. Humility comes from having the right perspective toward God and toward yourself. It has to do with who you trust. What do the following verses tell you about this?

Jeremiah 9:23-24

2 Corinthians 3:4-5

Philippians 2:3-4

What do you think is the difference between pride and confidence?

9. Read 1 Peter 5:5-6. Consider how God responds to the humble person. Why do you think God places such a high value on humility in a person's life?

What happens to people who humble themselves? Give an example from real life where someone who humbled himself was later exalted.

10. Read Romans 12:3.

   a. What do you think are the results of overestimating yourself?

   b. What do you think are the results of underestimating yourself?

Any preoccupation with self is pride.

PRIDE

Thinking too *highly* of self: "I do not want to trust God. God's work can't get along without me!"	Thinking too *lowly* of self: "I cannot trust God. God can't do anything through me!"

11. Meditate on Jesus' example of humility, trust, love, obedience, and exaltation from Philippians 2:5-11.

   a. Who did Jesus trust?

   b. How did Jesus exercise humility?

   c. What motivated Him to love so unselfishly?

   d. How did God the Father respond to Jesus' attitude?

12. Summarize the relationship you see between love and humility.

How would you articulate your own growth in love and humility?

LOVE IN SPEECH

13. How can loving words meet needs?

Proverbs 12:25

Isaiah 50:4

Ephesians 4:29

Colossians 4:6

14. How have you experienced verbal love from others? How do you typically respond to affirmation from others?

Who is someone you could love through kind, encouraging, or affirming words? What could you say?

15. What sins are you warned to avoid?

Proverbs 10:19

Proverbs 17:9

Proverbs 27:2

LOVE IN GOOD WORKS

Love is not just an inner feeling but also an act of the will. Love can be revealed by its effect on those who receive it. For a time it was popular to do "random acts of kindness." But expressing love through good works is always appropriate for a follower of Christ.

16. What is the relationship between salvation and good works? (Ephesians 2:8-10)

Why do you think followers of Jesus should do good works?

17. What should be the primary motivation behind your actions? (1 Corinthians 10:31)

18. Love Reality Check: Consider 1 John 3:17. Would you be willing to take off your coat and give it to a needy person? Perhaps you can think of an instance when you could have met another's need but did not. What can you do when another opportunity like this arises?

19. What should you remember in doing good works?

Galatians 6:9-10

Titus 3:8

Sometime ago a young soldier called his parents after his release from military service. He asked them if he could bring his buddy home with him. "You see, Mom, he said, "my friend was pretty badly wounded in battle. He has only one leg, one arm, and one eye."

After a long pause the mother said grudgingly, "Of course, son, he can stay with us a little while." Her voice, however, carried the message that they would not like to be burdened very long with such a severely handicapped person.

Two days later they received a telegram saying their son had plunged to his death from a hotel window. When his body arrived for burial, his mother was heartbroken, for he had only one leg, one arm, and one eye!

The memory of her last conversation still lingers with her, and she often cries out, "Oh, why didn't I speak more carefully, more lovingly? If I could only take back those selfish words, 'He can stay with us a little while.' But it is too late now!"

— Henry G. Bosch*

* Henry G. Bosch, *Our Daily Bread*, March 7, 1975.

1 Corinthians 13:13

And now these three remain: faith, hope and love. But the greatest of these is love.

1 Corinthians 13:13

This love of which I speak is slow to lose patience—it looks for a way of being constructive. It is not possessive: it is neither anxious to impress nor does it cherish inflated ideas of its own importance.

Love has good manners and does not pursue selfish advantage. It is not touchy. It does not keep account of evil or gloat over the wickedness of other people. On the contrary, it shares the joy of those who live by the truth.

Love knows no limit to its endurance, no end to its trust, no fading of its hope; it can outlast anything. (1 Corinthians 13:4-7, PH)

Write down how you like to be loved and how you like to demonstrate love.

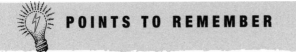

Add a sentence or two to the following statements to summarize the most important things you learned from each section of this chapter.

WHAT IS AUTHENTIC LOVE?

The Scriptures reveal and demonstrate God's unfailing love.

LOVING UNSELFISHLY

Love should be our hallmark as followers of Jesus.

LOVE IN HUMILITY

Trust is the starting point for love.

LOVE IN SPEECH

We demonstrate love by our kind words and affirmations.

LOVE IN GOOD WORKS

Actions will show the reality of our love.

The willingness to forgive others, to extend mercy to them, is a deep part of a character of love. Does your heart find it difficult to forgive others when they don't ask for forgiveness? That's where mercy and forgiveness do their greatest good. On the cross Jesus proclaimed, "Father, forgive them, for they do not know what they are doing" (Luke 23:34). Jesus offers mercy — not justice. Meditate on Matthew 6:14-15, Matthew 7:1-5, and James 2:12-13. Express your thoughts on forgiveness, judgment, and mercy — and how they relate to loving others.

3

Purity of Life

Living out the moral absolutes of God's Word is not easy or popular. In this world, many people seek freedom from all moral responsibility. Followers of Jesus have the privilege and obligation to live by biblical values. As we do, our confidence in God's goodness grows. We can experience more and more how God's will is "good, pleasing and perfect" (Romans 12:2).

1. Using a dictionary, define purity.

2. What does God promise to those who are pure in heart?
(Psalm 24:3-5; Matthew 5:8)

> **❝❝** Get as deep an impression upon your mind as is
> possible of the constant presence of the great and
> holy God. He is about our beds and about our
> paths and spies out all our ways. Whenever you are
> tempted to the commission of any sin, or the omis-
> sion of any duty, pause and say to yourself, "What
> am I about to do? God sees me."
>
> —Susanna Wesley to her eldest son, Samuel

3. What are some common impure behaviors to guard against?
(Ephesians 5:3-5)

4. The world's standards differ greatly from God's. From 1 John 2:15-16, what are some of the world's standards? List and define these.

Standard	Definition

5. Several New Testament passages state the characteristics of a person who is rightly related to others. Read 1 Timothy 5:1-2.

a. How are we to treat other people?

b. State at least two scriptural standards you have concerning your relationships with the opposite sex.

c. Is there any relationship you have that needs to be brought into conformity with these standards and attitudes? If so, what should you do about it?

THE IMPORTANCE OF PERSONAL PURITY

Although there are many arenas of personal purity, we will focus especially on the area of sexual purity and building godly relationships between men and women.

6. What are God's desires for our behavior?

Matthew 5:27-28

2 Corinthians 7:1

1 Thessalonians 4:3-8

Describe anything you are aware of that may be contaminating your body or spirit.

7. How does God describe those who practice impurity? (Ephesians 4:18-19)

8. List several reasons we should avoid immorality. (1 Corinthians 6:13-20; also see chart in the Going Deeper section.)

Verse 13

Verse 15

Verses 16-17

Verse 18

Verse 19

Verse 20

9. After God created the world and made male and female, He saw that it was good (Genesis 1:31). What are some reasons for our sexuality? (Genesis 1:27-28)

How can sexual immorality mess up God's good intentions?

10. What does Scripture say to the following excuses for immoral behavior?

a. "Since everyone does it, it must be all right." (see Proverbs 14:12)

b. "I just need to discover if this is right for me." (see Ecclesiastes 11:9)

c. "As long as I don't hurt anybody, it's okay." (see Leviticus 5:17)

d. "Nobody will ever find out that I did it." (see Hebrews 4:13)

e. "I'll stop after this one time." (see Galatians 6:7-8)

f. "I didn't really do anything; all I did was think about it." (see Matthew 5:28)

g. "If it feels pleasurable, it must be good." (see Hebrews 11:25)

THE PATH TO PURITY

Let's not kid ourselves. Remaining sexually pure in both thought and action is difficult. But it is not impossible!

11. What are the steps from temptation to sin? (James 1:14-15)

12. Read Genesis 3:6,8 and Joshua 7:21. How do these two passages compare? List the similarities.

	Genesis 3:6,8	Joshua 7:21
a. What physical sense was stimulated?		
b. What feeling resulted?		
c. What act resulted?		
d. What was done with the evidence?		

Do you think every act of sin follows this pattern? Why or why not?

13. Let's pause here for a moment. The world in which you live is likely filled with sexual images and opportunities. What do you think is the message sent out by the world about sex?

> The struggle is always going to be there. Since the Garden of Eden, humanity has been infused with the temptation to sin. What complicates the issue is the devious nature of porn. Porn is secret and seductive. It feeds off the lust nature of wanting more because "the eyes will never be satisfied." When we are struggling with a moral challenge, and especially if we have failed the test, our nature is to run and hide. Adam and Eve did the same thing — they tried to hide from God. . . . They tried to hide their sin the same way porn is hidden, creating the dirty little secret.

— Craig Gross and Mike Foster,
Questions You Can't Ask Your Mama About Sex

In light of God's desire for our purity, how does loving people and respecting their dignity apply to viewing pornography?

14. All of us have had different exposure and experience sexually, whether in real life or via pornography and the like. The Bible clearly assures us that there is no sin — even sexual sin — that God will not forgive. Based on the following Scripture, finish the statement, "No matter what I've done in the past, if I repent, God will forgive me because . . ."

Hebrews 9:14

Hebrews 10:19-23

15. Do you ever feel impure or dirty? If so, describe that feeling.

   a. Now, take a moment to imagine what it would feel like for you
      to be made clean and pure sexually. How much do you feel like
      you deserve this promised cleansing?

   b. What various emotions does this stir in your heart?

16. Try to forget the word *cat*. When you have forgotten it, check
    this box. ☐ Can you do it? This is how some people try to avoid

immorality. They think they can just make themselves not think about it. But it is impossible to eliminate a wrong thought from your mind unless you trust God to help you substitute something good in its place.

a. What is God's promise when facing temptation? (1 Corinthians 10:13)

b. Paul said that we are to "put off" the old nature and "put on" the new nature (Ephesians 4:22-24). This passage illustrates the essential principle of substitution. What is one practical way you can apply the substitution principle in your struggle for purity?

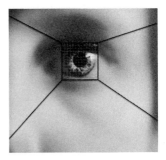

17. What can we do to live a clean life that is pleasing to the Lord?

Psalm 51:10

Proverbs 4:14-15

Romans 13:14

1 Peter 1:22

18. Study Genesis 39:7-12 and 2 Samuel 11:1-4. Compare the events in Joseph's and David's lives.

	Joseph	David
What were the surrounding circumstances?		
What were their respective attitudes?		
What were their resulting actions?		

Why do you think these two men responded in different ways to a similar situation?

PERSPECTIVE ON MARRIAGE

19. Read Genesis 2:18-25.

   a. Who originated marriage?

   b. For what purpose was marriage instituted?

   c. State the ideas of verse 24 in your own words.

20. Read 2 Corinthians 6:14-15.

   a. What principle does God set forth in this passage?

   b. How does this apply to a marriage?

c. What problems do you think a believer might face if this principle was violated?

21. What can you do if you are already in this kind of marriage? (1 Corinthians 7:12-16)

22. What possible reasons might there be for not marrying? (1 Corinthians 7:27-28,32-35)

23. Read Ephesians 5:21-33 — a passage on marriage.

a. What is God's desire for husbands, and what does this illustrate?

b. What is God's desire for wives, and what does this illustrate?

24. What is the desire of God's heart for His children as they live in the midst of a corrupt and depraved generation? (Philippians 2:15)

1 Timothy 5:1-2

Treat younger men as brothers, older women as mothers, and younger women as sisters, with absolute purity.

1 Timothy 5:1-2

In what areas of your life do you struggle with purity? Where do you think God is in your struggle with purity? Where would you like Him to be?

Add a sentence or two to the following statements to summarize the most important things you learned from each section of this chapter.

GOD'S STANDARD

God has definite standards for purity of thoughts, speech, and conduct.

THE IMPORTANCE OF PERSONAL PURITY

The Scriptures give clear reasons for maintaining personal purity.

THE PATH TO PURITY

God has provided principles and resources to help us in our struggle for purity.

PERSPECTIVE ON MARRIAGE

The Scriptures reveal God's perspective on purity in marriage.

In many cultures today, pornography and the media are attacking our purity. While the delivery systems are new, the struggle with sexual purity is an age-old struggle. The book of Proverbs (especially chapters 5–7) is packed with wisdom, warning, and advice about protecting our sexual purity. It warns us about the consequences and dangers of sexual sin.

Soberly consider these consequences of sexual sin based on Proverbs 5–7 in *The Message*.

Consequences of Sexual Sins

Proverbs 5	Proverbs 6:20-35	Proverbs 7
—like gravel in your mouth	—will eat you alive	—has you eating out of someone else's hand
—a pain in your gut	—like fire in your lap	—will bewitch you
—a wound in your heart	—you'll pay for it	—you are like a calf being led to a butcher shop
—headed straight for Hell	—soul-destroying	—you are like a stag lured into ambush
—no clue about Real Life	—self-destructive	—you are like a bird flying into a net
—squanders your life	—ruins your reputation	—makes you a victim
—exploited by those who care nothing for you	—detonates rage and revenge	—like a halfway house to hell
—ends in a life full of regrets	—nothing you say will make it all right	
—traps you in a dead end		
—rewards you with death		

Read one of the three chapters from Proverbs mentioned in the chart. From that chapter, what are some of the ways you can avoid being trapped by sexual sin? How can a close friend help? (Ecclesiastes 4:9-11)

> Cyber-sex is just another form of selfish sexual expression. It will leave you hanging—always wanting more and never satisfied. . . . Cyber-sex is dangerous because it often leads to more destructive forms of sexual expression. You may say to yourself, "No way, it won't happen to me," but you should read some of the e-mails we've received. People get more and more needy, and they find themselves getting deeper and deeper as they seek alternate forms of sexual gratification.
>
> —Craig Gross and Mike Foster,
> *Questions You Can't Ask Your Mama About Sex*

4

Integrity in Living

Living as a whole, integrated person can be challenging. We tend to put on masks, saying one thing but contradicting it by how we live. We struggle each day with issues of right versus wrong, good versus evil. We tend to rationalize our behavior and compromise God's standards of integrity. We may explain away or ignore these sins. These are the "vices of the virtuous" — sins that may have become accepted as the norm. But God is holy, and we must not allow any compromise with sin to infiltrate our lives. Because God is light, He will graciously reveal what we try to hide so that we can grow in integrity.

THE STRUGGLE FOR INTEGRITY

1. What did God say about the need for integrity, or honesty, when He gave the Ten Commandments? (Leviticus 19:11)

2. Read about Paul's struggle for integrity in Romans 7:15-20. In what ways can you identify with his struggle?

3. Read the familiar story of Adam and Eve's fall in Genesis 2:25–3:13. Number the following steps in the order they happened.

____ shame

____ disobedience

____ hiding

____ deception

____ fear

4. What are some ways we can be deceived?

   a. By ourselves

      James 1:22

      1 John 1:8

   b. By others

      Romans 16:17-18

      Ephesians 4:14

   c. By Satan

      Genesis 3:1

      2 Corinthians 11:3-4

> Authentic prayer calls us to rigorous honesty, to come out of hiding, to quit trying to seem impressive, to acknowledge our total dependence on God and the reality of our sinful situation. It is a moment of truth when defenses fall and the masks drop in an instinctive act of humility.
>
> —Brennan Manning, *Reflections for Ragamuffins*

5. Because we can be deceived so easily, how can we know when we have sinned or are improperly hiding?

Psalm 19:12

Psalm 139:23-24

Hebrews 4:12

6. Why is it a human tendency to hide? (John 3:19-21)

What does God's light do?

7. We must be careful to avoid hypocrisy. The Pharisees of Jesus' day were examples of how *not* to have integrity.

a. What did Jesus expose about hypocrites? (Mark 7:6-8)

b. What is one reason this style of living is dishonest? (Romans 2:23-24)

c. What is hypocritical about those described in 1 John 4:20?

8. Read Acts 5:1-5.

   a. Why do you think Ananias told this lie?

   b. Who was he lying to, and who influenced him to lie?

   c. Why do you think God took this so seriously?

9. Have you ever been lied to? How did you feel, and how did the lie impact your relationship with the person?

10. Our lives should be able to withstand close examination by other people. We should live honestly — not pretending to be something we are not in order to create a false impression. Imagine a mind-reading device that can project on a screen what a person is really like and what he or she is thinking.

a. Would you want this invention used on you?

b. Why or why not?

11. Consider the following list of common ways we can compromise our integrity. Which of these (if any) are problem areas for you?

___ living a double life

___ telling "white lies"

___ saying one thing but doing another

___ cheating

___ manipulating people's impressions of you

___ failing to keep promises

___ hiding for self-protection

___ illegally copying or downloading

___ (other) _____

>
> As a person of integrity, I no longer define myself by my sin or the sin committed against me, but by who God declares me to be.
>
> —Bill Thrall, Leadership Catalyst, Inc.

THE PRACTICE OF HONESTY

12. Read 1 Thessalonians 2:4-10. List several things that Paul's integrity prevented him from doing in his relationship with the people of Thessalonica.

13. Meditate on Acts 24:16 and 2 Corinthians 8:21. What are some practical ways you can keep your conscience clear before God and others?

14. Honesty should be displayed in all aspects of our lives. List below some of the areas we might neglect.

Romans 13:6-7

Colossians 3:23-25

1 Peter 2:13-14

Consider these two essential standards for honesty:

- *Make sure everything you own was obtained honestly.*
- *When you speak, speak the truth. There is no such thing as a "white lie."*

HONESTY IN SPEECH

15. What does your speech indicate? (Matthew 12:34-35)

Why do you think people cover up the truth about themselves?

16. Read James 3:8-10. What types of power does our speech have?

How does this illustrate our struggle for integrity?

17. We build trust in relationships
    through our integrity. And we
    erode trust through our dishonesty.
    Consider Proverbs 26:28. How could
    lying result in a lack of trust? How do
    you feel after someone lies to you?

    a. How have lies eroded your trust?

b. Think of a time when you did not tell the truth. How could you have come into the light of God's truth?

18. Any distortion of the truth — in word, exaggeration, actions, attitudes, or silence — is deceitful and a form of lying. Why are lying and abusive speech inconsistent with a life of following Jesus? (Colossians 3:8-10)

19. Paraphrase the following passages:

Ephesians 4:29

Colossians 4:6

20. Can you apply one of the verses in question 19 to a relationship with someone you know? What will you do? When will you do it?

> **Transparency is simply disclosing yourself to others. . . . In vulnerability, you deliberately place yourself under the influence of others. . . . You give them the right to know the pain of your weakness and to care for you. You choose to let others know you, to have access to your life, to teach you, and to influence you.**
>
> —Bill Thrall, Ken McElrath, and Bruce McNicol, *Beyond Your Best*

21. Read James 5:16 and consider the above quote from *Beyond Your Best*.

a. What would it look like for you to reveal yourself in your close relationships by being really honest about who you are and who you are not?

b. Describe a time when you were vulnerable (not simply transparent) about one of your weaknesses.

c. When, in humility, you put yourself under someone else's influence, what was the result?

SUGGESTED VERSE FOR MEDITATION AND MEMORIZATION

Ephesians 4:29

Do not let any unwholesome talk come out of your mouths, but only what is helpful for building others up according to their needs, that it may benefit those who listen.

Ephesians 4:29

The journey into integrity requires coming into the light — living truthfully as well as telling the truth. What has God been showing you through this study about your need to grow in integrity? Who do you trust to walk with you on your journey?

> The pursuit of godliness is not the pursuit of perfection but the pursuit of integrity and authenticity.
>
> —Bill Thrall, Leadership Catalyst, Inc.

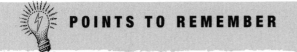

Add a sentence or two to the following statements to summarize the most important things you learned from each section of this chapter.

THE STRUGGLE FOR INTEGRITY

Deceit creates a struggle and exposes the need for integrity.

LACK OF INTEGRITY EXPOSED

Our goal is not a life of sinless perfection but rather a life that does not remain hidden.

THE PRACTICE OF HONESTY

God calls us to strive for a clear conscience before Him and others.

HONESTY IN SPEECH

Our speech exposes and expresses our heart.

Being honest to oneself is often difficult. Read Psalm 51:6. How are you speaking truth to yourself about your emotions, behaviors, identity, relationships, character, and so on? How is a spiritually mature person speaking truth into your life?

Why is this journey often difficult? How honest do you feel today?

Character Development in Suffering

If our character is like gold, we will not only need deep mining but also significant refining. God uses various processes to mature us by refining or purifying our character. Yet unresolved questions may stretch us: "Where is divine goodness in human misery? Why does God not stop pain, especially if it seems undeserved?"

A believer in Jesus is not immune to the experience of suffering and grief. Sickness, sorrow, death, disappointment, and pain are experienced by all people. When we as believers endure pain and suffering, we can find comfort and strength in God's promise that He is shaping His protective and sovereign purposes in us, and we can rest in our hope of glory in eternity.

GOD'S ULTIMATE CONTROL

1. What do the following verses teach about God's perspective and purpose?

   Isaiah 45:5-7

   Isaiah 46:9-11

   Do these truths about God's sovereignty comfort you or disturb you? Explain.

2. What did Joseph say about the difficult circumstances and troublesome people he faced? (Genesis 50:20)

3. Read Romans 8:18 and 8:28.

   a. What was Paul's attitude and conclusion?

b. How can these thoughts help you in all that you face?

4. Can you describe an experience in your life that at the time did not seem to be producing anything good yet later proved to be beneficial?

THE PURPOSE OF SUFFERING

5. Read Isaiah 52:13–53:12.

a. In what ways did Christ suffer unjustly?

b. How did He respond to this suffering? (53:7)

c. For whose sake did He endure this suffering? (53:8,11-12)

6. Now add to your answers to the previous three questions using 1 Peter 2:21-24.

How does Christ's suffering touch you? (verse 21)

7. What are some of the reasons God tested the children of Israel?

Deuteronomy 8:2-3

Deuteronomy 8:16

> God's wooing. It is the strange kiss of God, the reverse of the Judas kiss—a kiss to restore us and not to betray us. The pain becomes a narrow passage that leads down into a unique intimacy with the suffering servant.
>
> —Mark Buchanan, *Your God Is Too Safe*

8. What are some other ways God brings good from suffering?

John 15:2

Hebrews 12:6-7,10

1 Peter 1:6-7

How would you describe God's good
desire to develop and protect us?

> Grief is good. It is cleansing. It undoes my
> world—and that is the best part of it. I need to be
> undone; simply undone. No regrouping. We need
> to mourn; it is the only way our hearts can remain
> both free and alive in this world. Why? Because it,
> like nothing else, puts a stop to the constant striv-
> ing. Grief is the antidote to the incessant possessive
> demand within.
>
> —John Eldredge, *The Journey of Desire*

9. Reflect on Jesus' words in John 15:18-21.

   a. What does this reveal about the world's attitude toward God?

b. Why can we expect this response?

c. How do you feel about this reality?

YOUR RESPONSE TO SUFFERING

10. Read Luke 6:22-23 and 1 Peter 4:12-13.

    a. What types of suffering can we expect?

    b. How should this affect us both now and in the future?

11. Examine James 1:2-4.

    a. How can we be developed and matured by the difficulties we face?

b. Why is it so difficult to face trials with joy?

c. Why can we have confidence and trust in this process?

12. Consider John 16:33 along with 1 Peter 4:19. At the heart of enduring suffering is confidence and trust in God. What confidence do we have?

13. Read Ephesians 5:20 and 1 Thessalonians 5:18.

a. How does God want us to respond in every situation?

b. Why is this response important?

c. Sometimes our responses to suffering include anger, fear, shame, and other emotions. How can you be emotionally authentic and also thank God for suffering?

14. Read Philippians 1:12-21.

a. How did Paul suffer?

b. What was his attitude?

c. What were the results of his suffering?

15. What attitudes toward suffering were shown by the following men? The apostles: Acts 5:40-41

Stephen: Acts 7:59-60

Job: Job 1:20-22 (background in 1:6-19)

16. When you suffer, do you ever question God as Job did (3:11,20)?
Do you question His . . .

___ goodness

___ love

___ power

___ wisdom

___ delight in you

PRAYER PAUSE

Tell God you struggle with Him and ask Him to guide you into His loving heart that is jealous for you.

Our response to problems reveals our maturity level. Each crisis is an opportunity for character growth.

17. What do you think are some positive and negative ways we might respond in the midst of suffering?

Positive responses

Negative responses

What do our negative responses reveal?

18. Now look up the following passages to see what they add to your answer.

Romans 12:17-21

Hebrews 12:14-15

GROWING THROUGH SUFFERING

19. Read Romans 5:3-5. How can suffering develop us?

20. What can God's loving discipline produce in you?
    (Hebrews 12:10-11)

21. Read 2 Corinthians 1:3-4.

    a. What does this passage tell you about the benefits of suffering?

    b. Name a person you know who is presently going through a difficult time.

    c. What can you do to encourage this person?

> Apart from the presence of God, there is no deep healing for our grief. Time can make it easier, but that is all. The good news when our hearts are broken is that God invites us to freely mourn in the great space of His loving presence. Our pain does not threaten Him; it does not cause Him to fear that we will ruin His reputation. He is not repulsed with the ugliness we feel. Even when we hurt so much that we can hardly bear it, we are still His beloved.
>
> —Sally Breedlove, *Choosing Rest*

22. Meditate on Psalm 119:50,71,76 and this quote from *Choosing Rest*. How has suffering influenced your intimacy with God? How did the psalmist respond to suffering?

1 Peter 4:19

So then, those who suffer according to God's will should commit themselves to their faithful Creator and continue to do good.

1 Peter 4:19

Describe one painful experience or time of suffering for you. How has this experience deepened your walk with God? How can this experience help you encourage others?

Add a sentence or two to the following statements to summarize the most important points you learned from each section in this chapter.

GOD'S ULTIMATE CONTROL

God is in control of the circumstances surrounding us.

THE PURPOSE OF SUFFERING

We should expect to suffer and mature as a result.

YOUR RESPONSE TO SUFFERING

God wants us to learn to trust and offer thanks in all situations, even difficult ones.

GROWING THROUGH SUFFERING

Suffering can shape us for God's purposes.

Option A: Read Romans 8:17-25. As you consider the long-term perspective, do you feel that sharing in Christ's glory is worth the pain of sharing in His sufferings? Explain.

Option B: Because suffering is difficult to understand, we may hear confusing comments from others. Some may connect suffering to sin: "Your suffering must stem from some sin you have committed." Others may focus on the amount of faith you have: "If you had more faith, you could be healed." Still others may see the problem as related to not following God properly: "If the Holy Spirit was leading you, your problems would go away."

But are these approaches in line with God's Word? How does God want us to use pain?

Look at the biblically based ideas in the left column regarding difficulties. These are just examples of the positives that can come from suffering. Then in the right column, write briefly how this encourages you or any praise or thanks you want to express to God.

God's Desires for Us	Our Response
Trust We are clay (Isaiah 64:8); He is the Potter We are clay jars (2 Corinthians 4:7); He is powerful in us	
Strength We are weak (2 Corinthians 12:9-10); He gives strength	
Refinement and Maturity Suffering should develop us (Romans 5:3-5)	
No Fear We can be like a stressed tree that is fruitful (Jeremiah 17:8)	
Ministry We can comfort others (2 Corinthians 1:4) We can be an example of hope to others (1 Peter 3:14-15)	

THE ESSENTIAL BIBLE STUDY SERIES FOR TWENTY-FIRST-CENTURY FOLLOWERS OF CHRIST.

DFD 1
Your Life in Christ   1-60006-004-8

This concise, easy-to-follow Bible study reveals what it means to accept God's love for you, keep Christ at the center of your life, and live in the power of the Spirit.

DFD 2
The Spirit-Filled Follower of Jesus   1-60006-005-6

Learn what it means to be filled by the Spirit so that obedience, Bible study, prayer, fellowship, and witnessing become natural, meaningful aspects of your life.

DFD 3
Walking with Christ   1-60006-006-4

Learn five vital aspects to living as a strong and mature disciple of Christ through this easy-to-understand Bible study.

DFD 5
Foundations for Faith   1-60006-008-0

This compelling Bible study will help you get a disciple's perspective on God, His Word, the Holy Spirit, spiritual warfare, and Christ's return.

DFD 6
Growing in Discipleship   1-60006-009-9

This study will provide insight and encouragement to help you grow as a true disciple of Christ by learning to share the blessings you've received from God.

DFD 7
Our Hope in Christ   1-60006-010-2

In this study of 1 Thessalonians, discover how to undertake a comprehensive analysis of a book of the Bible and gain effective Bible study principles that will last a lifetime.

DFD Leader's Guide   1-60006-011-0

The leader's guide provides all the insight and information needed to share the essential truths of discipleship with others, whether one-on-one or in small groups.

Visit your local Christian bookstore, call NavPress at 1-800-366-7788, or log on to www.navpress.com to purchase.
To locate a Christian bookstore near you, call 1-800-991-7747.

NAVPRESS
BRINGING TRUTH TO LIFE
www.navpress.com